THE LYRIC IN THE LINES

POEMS

BY

JEAN HILL

Copyright © 2019. Jean Hill. All rights reserved

ISBN: 978-0-244-76625-2

Printed and Distributed by Lulu.com

First Published: March 2019

Second Edition

Other Work by **Jean Hill**

The Sting In The Tale
Poems and Short Stories

The Barb In The Rhyme

The Thorn In The Verse

Poems to make you laugh and cry

and

Let's Smile Again
**A Humorous Account of
Family Life in the Seventies**

Available from: Lulu.com
or
Amazon

Look Beyond the Clouds

STILL WRITING IT MY WAY

I've lost count of the number of times people have asked "When's book number five to be published?" – Well, here it is and I hope The Lyric in the Lines has been worth the wait. Is it really nearly five years since my first collection of poems saw print and some of them read out on Radio Berkshire? So much has happened since then.

I have met so many wonderful people, eaten so many dinners, lunches, teas and cakes at the presentations and never cease to be amazed at the enthusiasm and generosity of the audiences I have entertained. I well recall speaking to one group of senior citizens. A lady approached me afterwards saying, "Will you come along to my hundredth birthday party and entertain my guests with your poems?" 'Of course, I would be delighted', I replied – 'when is it?' "Oh", she said, "it's in four years' time but I want to make sure you'll be able to come". I am positive she will make her hundredth year – I just hope I'm still hanging on in there!

One gentleman (same audience) I will always remember. Speaking into the microphone I asked if everyone could hear me on the back row. "No", he shouted, "I can't hear a blinking word, but I like looking at you". My reply – 'Well, come and sit in the front, you'll have a better view'. Seeing as I'm no oil painting I took this as quite a compliment!

After one presentation I politely said 'Thank you for inviting me' to the organiser, who responded by saying "Yes, glad you were able to come; we really wanted a singer but you were cheaper". Oh, well, that's me – Mrs Average from the Bargain Basement. 'Tell the truth and shame the devil' – as my Granny used to say.

I've had the opportunity to meet and talk with people from all walks of life. I've interacted with the views of the young, the confidence of those in middle age, and the wisdom of years that only the old can share. If I've learnt one thing during the past few years it's never let age cloud ambition. It's all been a privilege.

The Sting in the Tale, The Barb in the Rhyme, The Thorn in the Verse and Let's Smile Again continue to thrive and make people laugh. Available from Lulu.com and Amazon, and bookshops on request.

I hope you enjoy reading The Lyric in the Lines as much as I have enjoyed writing it. A huge Thank-You to all my friends who have supported me from the beginning, and to you, the reader, who has become so special – I couldn't have done it without you.

ACKNOWLEDGEMENTS

Deborah and **Samantha** … for being so hugely supportive in the practical production of this fifth book.
Without your skill and patience it would never have happened.

Sharon … for continued encouragement.

Robin … for the front cover photography.

Benjamin and **Jamie** … for just being.

The talented members of Wokingham Library Poetry Group for never-ending inspiration.

My friends Hélène and Tom
for giving me the lilac for the front cover photograph from their beautiful garden.

THANK–YOU ALL

The Sun is Always Shining

A BULL CALLED KEITH

Daisy, me and Buttercup
Live in a field of green
We are the fairest heifers
The world has ever seen

The farmer wants some calves next year
And we're all for procreation
But we don't fancy Keith – our bull
Or artificial insemination

Keith is such a pretty bull
But in our bovine way
We think he fancies Arthur
Who's 'come out' – or so they say

Arthur's quite a pedigree
And bursting with credentials
He flashes all his assets
And flaunts all his essentials

Keith's bought a tin of Brasso
The ring through his nose he's polished
And any thoughts the farmer has
Will have to be abolished

We calmly 'moo' and swish our tails
And chew the cud each day
And gently laugh at Farmer Brown
Who's bought a bull that's gay

A 'FIVE-A-DAY' PLAN

Do you struggle with the 'five-a-day'
We need to eat to keep us well
Now I've a little secret
And to you, my friend, I'll tell

The first of five is easy
We all like a G & T
Chuck in a slice of **lemon**
And we'll be drinking healthily

They tell us we should eat more veg
And to make your taste buds tingle
You get one of your 'five-a-day'
With a cheese and **onion** Pringle

So now you've got the hang of it
A scoop of **Raspberry** Ripple
But to boost your daily quota
You can make that scoop a triple

Throw in a glass of wine or two
(Can't have too many **grapes**)
This diet's really simple
You can share it with your mates

With energy levels bursting
You'll not get in a rut
With all the benefits in a bar
Of Cadbury's **fruit** and **nut**

Yes, I'll stick to healthy options
And now I've had my say
I'll throw in a Chocolate **Orange**
And double up to 'ten-a-day'

AMEN TO THAT

Our Master, who art in Brussels
Avarice be thy name
Thy Union come
And we will be done
In Britain as it is in Europe
Give us this day our country back
And forgive us our aversion
As we forgive those who take our billions
And lead us not up the garden path
But deliver us from greed
For thine is the 'gravy train'
The power and rapacity
For never and never
Amen

AWAKENING

The whisper of a spring-time breeze
Blackbirds singing in the oak
As the earth shakes off the mantle
Of its cold and frosty cloak

See greening shoots and hazy sun
Heads of crocus fill the lawn
Rays of warmth to touch the ground
Sparkle in the dew-drenched dawn

The squirrel nesting in its drey
Its kittens snug within
Waiting for the summer-time
And a new life to begin

The changing of the seasons
The sun in ascent climbs
As it was in the beginning
And will be 'til end of time

BITTER-SWEET

Was it just last Christmas
When you left me high and dry
The year has passed in just a flash
And I've long since ceased to cry

You left me then for greener grass
But for every blade you sow
You'll find a weedy tangle
Which now you have to mow

Your Christmas card was wistful
But I think it's quite ironic
Instead of quiet retirement
You're knee-deep in sick and colic

'Cos your new wife's had a baby
And I'm delighted now to know
You'll re-visit skills of parenting
Left behind so long ago

Think of poo filled nappies
And all the sleep you'll lose
The dribble down your shirt-front
And good luck with 'baby-blues'

And what of all the years ahead
With play-dough in your hair
You'll have to ditch the sports-car
For a hatchback you can share

No quiet sherry in the garden
Leisure lunches in the pub
There'll be homework, cubs and brownies
Football and swimming club

And when your wife presents you
With babies two or more
Don't come to me for sympathy
I've firmly shut that door

Just think of teenage tantrums
In their adolescent years
And your wife all menopausal
Screeching through her temper tears

So your life's not a bed of roses
And old times you can't forget
Do I read between your written words
Reminiscence and regret

But in candle glow, with crackling fire
Christmas cake and glass of wine
Good book, mince pie and perfect peace
Don't you worry, I'm just fine

Your armchair may stand empty
But I can't say that I care
And of your pension, dearest
I'll make sure I get my share

So Happy Christmas, sweetie-pie
Now I'm in charge of the remote
I'll watch 'weepies' on the telly
And just sit here and gloat!

BLACK FRIDAY

The Americans are funny
They like tradition quite a lot
Each year they have Thanksgiving
To thank the Lord for all they've got

And then they have Black Friday
And this they can't ignore
They join in the demented throng
To try and grab some more

BLAME BREXIT

Have you heard the weather forecast
'Unprecedented snow'
With blizzards and a hurricane
The Artic winds will blow
With rain and hail and freezing fog
Trapped in winter's vice
Frost on every window-pane
Pavements thick with ice

The temperature will plummet
Zero – less a score
And it's all the fault of Brexit
And European Law
In all the argy-bargy
We didn't heed their warning
And now they've gone and cancelled
Our share of Global Warming

BREXIT BLACKMAIL

2017

See how the EU bully boys
Are mapping out the course
As Brexit trails the rocky road
On the path to our 'divorce'
Now that Jean-Claude Juncker
Perched on his 'gravy train'
Is demanding British billions
To pour down Europe's drain

I've seen them on the telly
The Gallic shoulder shrug
Couldn't we return to them
A German doodlebug
They're fleecing this poor island
This green and sovereign isle
With arrogance and avarice
The European style

Your thoughts may not agree with mine
My view you may decry
We all fought for democracy
'Though sometimes I wonder why
Each with their own agenda
And democratic right
But we're ***all*** just sick and tired of
This endless Brexit fight

So as in long past conflicts
This island stands alone
With the threat of a recession
Please don't pare us to the bone
I'm just your Mrs Average
Oh, yes, I voted Brexit
And if our Government's got muscle
Then now's the time to flex it

BRITS ABROAD

There's nothing more alluring
Than the average Brit abroad
Two weeks in the sunshine
That he sees as his reward
For months of toil and trouble
Under England's sky of grey
He's out to have a good time
On his annual holiday

There are Germans and Italians
But this Brit – he flies the flag
With elastic socks and sandals
And a plastic shopping bag
He doesn't like the foreign food
Prefers a 'Triple Mac'
And sits around all blistered red
With sun-cream on his back

With belly bared protruding
Glistening proudly in the sun
Shorts pulled down an inch or two
He flaunts his manly 'builders bum'
Epitomizing British manhood
While shooting off his mouth
Is he from 'North of Watford'
Or a 'softie' from the South

He goes for 'all-inclusive'
Drinks beer with Coco-Pops
Then staggers to the beach bar
And on a plastic lounger flops
There to spend his holiday
His two weeks break in Spain
Before he boards an Easy-Jet
And flies back home again.

CHARITY BIRTHDAY

On your special day each year
My thoughts turn just to you
I know your birthday's getting near
And to forget it wouldn't do

As the day approaches
A present I must buy
I walk round shops and scratch my head
And come out with a sigh

The gifts are too expensive
I want to buy you something nice
I know that it's the thought that counts
But I can't afford the price

So to the local Charity Shop
To find a gift that's right
With under-wear and over-wear
And garments such a sight

There were undies all with holes
And there were jumpers full of moth
Pairs of shoes that had no soles
And lots of hats made out of cloth

I came out with quite a bundle
You ought to be so pleased
The total cost was fifty pence
For the load that I had seized

Now I've arranged a celebration
We'll dress as tramps and have a ball
And you'll be the most authentic
The best-dressed vagabond of all

So I'll see you at the party
Your present to deliver
I hope you'll have a happy day
That will go on forever

CHEESY CHOICES

All the mice sat round the great table
In Hamelin's impressive Guildhall
To discuss the best cheese selection
For the Pied Piper's Christmas Eve ball

Wilfred chaired the great Council meeting
And spoke with his best squeaky voice
As he handed each member the menu
And asked each mouse to make a first choice

Said Terrence, the town mouse, from Tooting
You can't beat a strong Gorgonzola
With fresh crusty bread and some pickles
Washed down with a cold Pepsi-Cola

Then Freda, a field mouse, from Farnham
Said my vote's for a nice creamy Brie
It's maybe a touch continental
But goes well with a hot cup of tea

But Grenville, grey house mouse, from Greenwich
Timid and shy had a hunch
To select a good mature Cheddar
They could melt it on toast for their lunch

Monty, white mouse, from the Manor
Whiskers bristling roared out that they ought
To consider an oak-ripened Stilton
To eat after dinner with port

Then Dotty, a dormouse, from Dorset
Said I must promote Parmesan
It's not eaten neat on cream-crackers
But sprinkled on pasta with ham

Poor Maurice, church mouse, from St. Michael
Too pious to let down his hair
Humbly squeaked from the corner
That he'd choose a rich Camembert

Red Leicester, Edam and Blue Danish
Soft white cheese from old nanny goats
All suggestions were put on the table
And the Council of Mice cast their votes

Then Wilfred wound up the proceedings
With a smile and all whiskers a-twitch
Time now to adjourn for our dinner
The winning vote was for Cod and Chips

CHRISTMAS AFTERMATH

Glitter in the carpet, nut shells in the vac
Take the fairy lights and tinsel off the tree
Search for all the receipts, take the presents back
Check the broken toys are under guarantee
Give the cat the giblets, make a turkey stew
Finish off the sherry and the Bailey's too
Credit card is maxed out, Christmas done and gone
Just twelve months before the next one comes along

This type of poem is called a Rispetto (Italian)
To follow the discipline, lines 1 & 3 and 2 & 4 must rhyme;
as do lines 5 & 6 and 7 & 8.
The difficult bit is that each line must
contain exactly eleven syllables.

COMEUPPANCE

'What a tangled web we weave
When we first practice to deceive'
And if with illicit love you are afire
Let me tell you hubby dear
Retribution day draws near
You're going to get much more than you desire

I saw her husband on the telly
He's all muscle, arms and belly
He's a wrestler called Mick the Maniac
And so I must confess
I gave him your address
And now he's breathing fire for the attack

And for your *ménage à trois*
He'll have you pickled in a jar
Quiet reasoning has never been his thing
And for your love life tangled
Mad Mick will have you mangled
And I think that you'll regret your mid-life fling

Now for your re-assurance
I've checked out your life-insurance
There isn't room for doubt or compromise
You can keep your bimbo-floozy
It's my turn to be choosey
And a fortune will be mine at your demise

COUNCILLORS PICNIC

(Sing to the tune of The Teddy Bears Picnic)

If you go down to the town today
You're sure of a big surprise
Go to Wokingham Town today
You'll never believe your eyes

For every shop that ever there was
Has now closed down forever because
Today's the day the councillors
Eat their picnic

See the workmen shovelling
The developers are having a lovely time today
Watch them, catch them unawares
And see them pocket council tax we pay

See the councillors splash the cash
To cover up the hash
They never have any care
The time will come when residents here
Refuse to pay their rates for a year
And that's the time they'll all choke on their picnic

For every councillor who's approved
Is sure of a treat today
There's lots of marvellous trees to fell
And vandalous games to play

Beneath the trees where nobody sees
They'll hide and scheme as long as they please
'Cause that's the way
The councillors like their picnic

Watch the workmen laying pipes
The contractors are having a lovely time today
Pavements catch us unawares
As through the maze we find our weary way

See us try to walk the plank
Find the entrance to bank
We tread each step with care
And with every month that passes by
The Wokingham residents wonder why
We let the councillors have their blooming picnic

Written to illustrate the feelings of local residents during the 'regeneration' of Wokingham which was once our lovely market town

COWPATS

Have you heard the latest
Read on the news just now
The total cause of climate change
Is all down to the cow

Their gaseous emissions
Have stirred up quite a stink
And for scientific research
It provides the missing link

Now as they slowly chew the cud
In meadows, fields and hills
There – steaming in the cowpats
You'll find indigestion pills

DEFLECTIONS OF MOONLIGHT

The shimmering light through silhouette trees
Shivering leaves on a whispering breeze
Mystical beam of the moon's ghostly shaft
On glittering water – a clear silver path

But like life's journey, one ripple disturbs
No clear way forward, the pathways diverge
Through silent dark trees and black water lake
Whirlpools of circumstance – which path should you take

DUTY

I've never been a royalist
But give the Queen her due
She flies the flag for Britain
Even though she's ninety-two

So in line with royal protocol
With elegance and grace
She met the U.S. president
With a greeting on her face

She kept her thoughts quite private
But her heart gave a downward thump
Tea with 'Barbie Doll' Melania
And the odious Donald Trump

But with a smile of welcome
British to the core
Our Queen still did her duty
And entertained this bore

We've seen he has no manners
And arrogant is his talk
Did he slurp tea from his saucer
Can be use a pastry fork

Did he bow his head politely
Say "Thanks for having me"
Did he appreciate the honour of
The Queen inviting him to tea

I hope with age she will forget
That in her reign's long span
The day she had to take her tea
With this pompous loud-mouth man

EVIL CREATION

'All Things Bright and Beautiful
All Creatures Great and Small'
How we sweetly sang those words
In the school's assembly hall

But surely God's regretting
In this cruel world He created
Where predators hunt the weakest
And the bloodlust urge is sated

How trite the saying, glib the words
His plan lacked one small item
Bigger fish eat little fish
And so ad infinitum

With man the perpetrator
Of trophy hunting just for thrills
As he raises up his shotgun
And without compassion kills

So, God, in your wisdom
(And of that I'm not so sure)
Can't you redress the balance
In the name of nature's law

Let the elephant charge the hunter
Let the lion get in first bite
And in the name of justice
Let's make this a fairer fight

Let the bullet miss the zebra
Rebound and ricochet
Right through the hearts of hunters
To even up a sporting day

Let the pheasant not grace tables
Of the rich and inhumane
And let the deer roam boldly
In our countryside again

Let the dolphin net the fisherman
Watch him flounder in the brine
And let the animal kingdom
Rejoice with vengeance thine

Real men shoot with cameras
No need to prove they're brave
They leave that to the hunters
The inadequate and depraved

FOR GOD'S SAKE

Dear God, I'm a mere mortal
Stood despairing at your portal
Please listen to my words for what they're worth
We know the skies you govern
And send some to Satan's oven
But what we want is retribution here on earth

Now I may be without merit
And the world I won't inherit
But can't you see that thy will isn't done
There are murderers and muggers
And other thieving buggers
Who cause havoc and destruction just for fun

Although a lowly minion
I will give you my opinion
On gibbets up the high street hang the lot
Let bombers without reason
Face the penalty of treason
Stand them up against the wall and have them shot

Forget about forgiving
We want justice for the living
And let me tell you, God, we're on the brink
Take a look at your creation
And strike evil from each nation
Or are you not as powerful as we think

Thugs don't do repentance
Meter out a lengthy sentence
Or will you forget and turn the other cheek
Why don't you get cracking
And arrange for them a smacking
And get on with the protection of the weak

In forty days and forty nights
I could put the world to rights
I've talked it through with all the mates I've got
And although vengeance is thine
We'd make punishment fit the crime
And spifflicate the flaming rotten lot

I know I'm a curmudgeon
Who's speaking in high dudgeon
But what happened to those chariots of flame
How about a locust plague
And pestilence for the depraved
Then we'd all walk in your image once again

Don't put me asunder
I don't want to steal your thunder
But it isn't going smoothly as you planned
Just let me say, forsooth
Take eye for eye and tooth for tooth
Before the blooming lot gets out of hand

Dear God, I'll wave your banner
If you'd just put a spanner
In the scheming hearts of all the violent men
I'd be cheering at their slaughter
You could hang and draw and quarter
And we'd all sleep safer in our beds again

For heavenly comeuppance
We don't give an earthly tuppence
It's settling the score *here* we applaud
So smite down all the sinners
Let the righteous be the winners
And grant us peace on earth again dear Lord

FUTILITY

'I clasp my children and shield them with my body
My world explodes and the city is aflame
My prayers to God for protection go unanswered
London 1940 – and still the bombers come'

'I clasp my children and shield them with my body
My world explodes and the city is aflame
My prayers to Allah for protection go unanswered
Syria 2020 – and still the bombers come'

Throughout ages, these conflicts – eighty years between
Brown eyes, blue eyes, across aeons of time unite in fear
Nothing changes, no-one cares, no lessons clear
No omnipotent power will intervene

A slaughter of the innocent – an evil unfurled
A world choked by the delirium of war
A penetrating madness in whatever land or foreign shore
Still Hell pervades our blood-stained world

GOOD OLD DAYS

Yes, I remember the good old days
The chilblains on my feet
The chilling cold of lino floors
To shock you from your sleep

Yes, I remember the good old days
Ice on each window pane
The damp patch on the ceiling
That dripped water in the rain

Yes, I remember the good old days
And fetid blocked-up drains
Freezing huts in dank back yards
The toilet's rusty cistern chain

Yes, I remember the good old days
When polio was rife
Scarlet fever and diphtheria
Claimed many a poor child's life

Yes, I remember the good old days
When the word 'obey' was said
And women became chattel
From the day that they were wed

Yes, I remember the good old days
The lucky few – and those
Who look back with nostalgia
Through spectacles tinted rose

Yes, I remember the good old days
When birth and death soon met
But if it's all the same to you
I'd rather just forget

HEARTFELT WISH

We all know that obesity
Can lead to heart attacks
So why don't we cut the sugars
And the saturated fats

We know we must keep active
Take lots of exercise
Before we block our arteries
And our heart gives up and dies

Everyone knows smoking
(There's a warning on each pack)
Will lead us to an early grave
With stroke or heart attack

So let's treat our hearts kindly
Not leave it to the NHS
Let's look at our *own* life-style
And our bodies re-assess

JUST SIGN THE PRE-NUP DARLING

My dear it's you I cherish
And our love will never perish
We'll make a vow for better or for worse
What's yours is mine, of course
But if it comes to a divorce
What's mine is mine, so sign the pre-nup first

My dear our love won't falter
As you lead me to the altar
And all your worldly goods you me endow
In sickness and in health
I'll gladly share your wealth
But dearest will you sign the pre-nup now

The prenuptial arrangement
In case of an estrangement
Is a blessing and a boon in a disguise
But if you'll kindly think it through
Then I'll gladly say "I do"
So sign the pre-nup sweetheart I'd advise

While you're anticipating
And I am contemplating
Our life will be one of eternal bliss
There's the place to sign
Put your moniker on the line
And I'll seal the pre-nup darling with a kiss

MEMORIES

(ACROSTIC)

Meandering back through long ago days
Evocative scenes the memory plays
Music and laughter, we danced in the sun
Once when we lived the life of the young
Recall, recapture the joy of our youth
Indelibly etched now we're long in the tooth
Elusive memories, quicksilver, moonbeams
Soon, all too soon, all that's left is our dreams

Grasp every opportunity
A memory to create
Greet each day with fun and gladness
With love and laughter radiate

When my time on earth is through
Before they close the lid
I don't want to say 'I wish I had'
I want to say 'I'm glad I did'

<u>MY AUNTIE JANET</u>

I've studied Global Warming
But Science has it wrong
It's not down to the poor old cow
With their ripe effluvial pong

Although she breaks wind gently
And discreetly as she can
The hole in the ozone layer
Is caused by my Auntie Jan

She quaffs down pints of lager
And although it makes her queasy
She'll tuck in with great relish
To a fiery prawn Jalfrezi

She likes baked beans and curry
And sure enough they gives her gas
But Friday nights you'll find her
Scoffing blistering Madras

So with a spicy poppadom
The destruction of this planet
Is down to red-hot Vindaloo
And my dear old Auntie Janet

MY SILENT WORLD

The curtains are edged with light
But no chorus heralds my dawn
No birdsong welcomes the end of night
No wakening sounds that would delight
Me – to hear the world re-born

The radio on – the volume turned high
The words are just a muffled sound
The news and forecast – they pass me by
And the world events still mystify
Me – with mutterings confound

The gentle whisper of a summer breeze
The tinkling splash of a waterfall
The rustling leaves on autumn trees
No longer will these senses please
Me – just a memory to recall

No hum and whoosh on the motorway
No throbbing roar from the 'plane above
No background music in a store's café
No noise as laughing children play
Me – missing all the sounds I love

Around the table I see people smile
I arrange my face in similar vein
Not understanding and know that I'll
Feel isolation all the while
Me – knowing I'll not hear again

I speak but get the context wrong
Your spoken words I can't unfurl
And if I feel your patience gone
I don't belong – devoid of song
Me – in my silent world

NEIGHBOURS NEW YEAR'S EVE PARTY

I'm going to a party
A small gathering, quite select
To welcome in the New Year
And on the old one to reflect

The neighbours have invited me
To mix and match and mingle
While scooping guacamole
On a cheese and onion Pringle

Food's not bad, I have to say
There's a pâté made of kipper
And these chopped-up carrot wedges
Make a tasty little dipper

There's swanky cut-glass dishes
With olive oil in patterned swirl
Floating on balsamic vinegar
With a bread-stick you can twirl

For those without sophistication
There's twiglets, nuts and crisps
Tortilla Chips and Nachos
And sausages on sticks

Now I'm not one to gossip
And I never criticize
But have you seen the 'sell-by' date
On this packet of mince pies

And have you tried the sausage rolls
I think they come from Lidl
There's lots of flaky pastry
But not much sausage in the middle

I see the vicar's been invited
Face 'holier than thine'
Slipping shots of vodka
In the church communion wine

There's the Browns from Number Two
He gets right on my wick
Double dipping in the hummus
With his stringy celery stick

Can't say I'm too keen on her
I've seen her at the bottle bank
Chucking in gin bottles
Pissed as a newt – thick as a plank

See the Jeffries there from down the road
By the salsa and cucumber
Think they're posh 'cos their house has
A name and not a number

But I don't speak to the Joneses
She's a tart and he's a louse
She's all 'red hat and no knickers'
And they've got a bigger house

I've not met that couple over there
But rumour says they're Swiss
Their eldest son has acne
And is growing cannabis

Don't look now – there's man-mad Maureen
Her – with the crazy-paving drive
She eyeing Fred with his allotment
For husband Number Five

There's Doris Grimm – she's on the council
With husband Donald – he's a drip
Now Maureen's dropped an earring
In the avocado dip

I'll have to talk to Mrs Frobisher
She's just had grand-child number six
They've all got different fathers
Her daughter's into 'Pick 'n Mix'

And have you seen the Fredericks
Her nets are a disgrace
And with the state their garden's in
I'm surprised they show their face

They've invited those new neighbours
I don't know where they're from
But when they're cooking curry
It don't half cause a pong

Look there's Mrs What's 'er Name
With her ugly husband, Sam
You can see she's piled the weight on
And she's mutton dressed as lamb

As twelve strikes I'll dodge the kissing
Out manoeuvre Ernie Blogg
With nostril hair and halitosis
I'd rather kiss his dog

But I'll smile and sip Prosecco
Join the jolly bonhomie
And pick the needles out my jumper
From their moulting Christmas tree

Yes, I guess it's a tradition
And to party is a must
But come the stroke of midnight
Then they won't see me for dust

I'll thank the hosts politely
Wish them hale and hearty cheer
Then make sure I avoid them
For another blooming year

NO NUDISTS IN EASTBOURNE

No, they don't have nudists in Eastbourne
Not like those on French foreign shores
Where the men just wear layers of sun-cream
And the women prance round without drawers

Eastbourne's a place of refinement
'Though we're all over sixty, it's true
With cardies and blouses and grey hair
That the posh have all tinged silver-blue

It's the home of the crimplene floral
With wide fitting sandals and flats
And our stockings are elasticated
And we all carry plastic rain hats

We'll sit on a bench on the sea-front
And suffer our aches and our pains
We'll discuss in hushed tones all our ailments
And show off our varicose veins

And if we want a day of excitement
A coach-trip to see Beachy Head
But we'll be back by three for afternoon tea
And by ten we'll be tucked up in bed

No, we don't have nudists in Eastbourne
And if you consider the facts
The breeze would freeze their essentials
And the pebbles would pattern their backs

We'll rest on the front by the flower-beds
And think of the money we save
We'll keep this resort for the old folk
And those with one foot in the grave

OLIVE TREE

Sunlight, sunlight, dance for me
The grey-green leaves of the olive tree
Seeped in mystical magic sway
From biblical times to modern day
The sun-kissed emblem of ancient Greece
Stalwart legend through war and peace

With clustered flower of pearly sheen
In axils of the evergreen
And gnarled trunks deep in dusty soil
Give blackened fruit and golden oil
In sunlight's shadow shelter me
As I sit and dream 'neath the olive tree

PANCAKE DAY

It's Pancake Day on Tuesday
And a predicament I'm in
I'm hopeless at this cooking lark
Just don't know how to begin

I've searched on line for recipes
And found one by Nigella
How to make the perfect pancake
And spread it with Nutella

For tea I'd make a sweet one
With dairy cream and jam
Or perhaps – for lunch – a savoury
Rolled up with cheese and ham

So I sifted very carefully
The lumps out of the flour
Then cracked in the eggs and milk
And turned the beater on full power

The mixture flew in all directions
On walls and ceiling spread
And as I cleaned the mess up
I won't tell you what I said

So if at first you don't succeed
Do I give up – not me – Oh No
I turn the beater speed right down
And have another go

I poured my mix into the pan
But there it stuck like glue
I scraped if off in blackened chunks
With a Brillo Pad or two

To make a blooming pancake
To watch the batter set and fry
The gas is on, the pan is greased
Let's have another try

Well, the pancake browned quite nicely
So I tossed it in the air
It got caught in the ceiling fan
And bits fell in my hair

My last attempt – a final fling
The gas flame's burning bright
I poured some oil into the pan
And the batter mix caught light

The smoke poured out the window
And the fire brigade arrived
With all the flames and burning oil
It's a wonder I survived

Yes, I know that it's Shrove Tuesday
And pancakes would be nice
But wouldn't you like noodles
And a plate of egg-fried rice

This is one tradition
That's beyond my expertise
I'll ring up for some crispy duck
And we'll have a nice Chinese

PEA BRAIN PENALTY

We've been here on the Isle of Wight
And quite enjoyed our stay
'Til the idiot Parking Warden
Went and ruined our nice day

To be a Parking Warden
You don't need a good degree
In fact you only have to have
The brain power of a pea

The notice-board – it clearly said
Park where the coaches go
So there we parked our motorhome
With two-hour ticket placed on show

We found the rules and regulations
And every word we read
'Motorhomes in Coach Bay'
And we parked – just like it said

So why have we a parking fine
We've not stayed over long
Can the twerp not read the board
Just what have we done wrong

Perhaps the warden should have gone
As the advert does suggest
For an appointment at SpecSavers
To have an eyesight test

But let me tell you by this missive
Just be sure that I'm not bluffing
You can put your parking ticket
Where the turkey puts his stuffing

Or dear Council of the Island
Let's plant an evolutionary seed
Please test your Parking Wardens
On their ability to read

'PHONING SUSAN

We ignored all the arguments
Told her not to make a fuss
We decided that the time had come
To have Mother live with us

We'll manage all her finance
And as legal legatee
Make sure that our inheritance
Wings its way to me

So we turned around the box-room
Signed her up for Medicare
Bought a bedspread made of candlewick
And an orthopaedic chair

She'll sit by the radiator
In a quilted dressing-gown
We'll keep Velcro slippers by the fire
For if we have to ask her down

You'd think she'd be quite grateful
Appreciate our sacrifice
But she threw her dinner at me
Followed by her prunes and rice

I'm at the end of my tether
I don't know what to do
We need a family conference
So I'll ring my sister, Sue

"What shall we do about Mother
Her mind's flipped, her virtue gone
She went to that Ann Summers shop
And bought herself a thong

She's found herself a toy-boy
They're dancing in her room
Can you hear the music down the 'phone
My head's vibrating with the boom

I don't like the bloke she's taken with
He's got earrings – quite uncouth
She's like a teenager re-cycled
And he's revived his mis-spent youth

They're upsetting all the neighbours
As last night at half-past two
They staggered up the driveway
I could tell they'd had a few

She's bought eyelash extensions
Grown a fringe and had it lightened
Now she's ringing up the dentist
To have her false teeth whitened

They're going off on holiday
No, not Eastbourne by the sea
If they just planned to sit in shelters
I'd be more likely to agree

No, they've booked a Caribbean cruise
It's caused a lot of trouble
Not for them two single cabins
They've gone and booked a double

The situation's getting urgent
We must prove her mind's unsound
She's spending all her money
So I got the doctor round

She's taken back her pension book
And they're making out new wills
Now she's poured gin into her cocoa
And won't take her sleeping pills

I felt medical opinion
Would provide a bit of hope
That's before she told the doctor
Where to stuff his stethoscope

I thought I'd better ring you
To get this off my chest
Now you won't believe this, Sue
She's chucked out her thermal vest

She's bought herself some 'leathers'
Doesn't care that she's a sight
In a fluorescent helmet
She's riding pillion on his bike

Last night they went out clubbing
Disco-danced 'til after one
And, Sue, it isn't seemly
For old folk to have such fun

I'd like to have her grounded
Turn the key and lock her in
She said she'd contact Age Concern
And found the number where to ring

She's had her toenails polished
Now she's gone beyond the pale
She's the only old age pensioner
With a blue-rinsed ponytail

And she's gone vegetarian
She's out there hugging trees
And he's into Morris Dancing
With bells tied round his knees

Yes, I might be menopausal
And hysteria is looming
But Sue – this is our mother
That this gigolo is grooming

But now this is the last straw
The one that broke the camel's back
She's got herself a tattoo
And I'm sure they're snorting 'smack'

Mother's gone quite loopy
Don't know what Dad would have said
Can you hear that thump and twanging
It's the bedsprings on her bed

I'm going to barge right in there
I'm going to shout and rave
This house will know no peace again
Until she's in her grave

Now I've got to 'phone the vicar
Get him here quick as he can
Mother's just informed me
She's ripped up her funeral plan

Sue, Susan, are you listening
Can you have Mother there
She's driving me quite mental
And I'm tearing out my hair

I can't cope any longer
My nervous breakdown's overdue
I'm evicting Mother and her lover
They can come and live with you

Now Sue please don't be horrid
To say I've feathered my own nest
You know I care for Mother
And acted for the best

I can't believe you find this funny ….."
What's that buzz – the dialling tone
My heartless sister Susan
Has hung up the flaming 'phone

POWER OF THE PEN

History can't turn back the pages
The future's still there to be written
From the sad Brexit betrayal
Let's fly the flag for Britain

Put some more ink in your pen
(Just make sure that it's blue)
And write to every politician
And tell them what to do

The past won't be forgotten
Now's the time to come out fighting
So sharpen up your pencils
Turn a clean page and start writing

PRECIOUS HARVEST

There's a little school in Kensal Rise
At the end of Harvist Road
It stands between the craters
Where the bombers dropped their load

In a landscape scarred with tragedy
As they walk to school each day
Children climb across the bomb-site
And make up games to play

They scramble through the rubble
And deprived of childhood toys
Bang – Bang – they shoot each other
And play at Soldier Boys

All poorly clad in hand-me-downs
And boots with holes re-heeled
Given just one precious gift
'Though love's a fragile shield

In this our Britain's darkest hour
We thank the stars above
For all the blessed children
That are the harvest born of love

And fear haunts every mother
That one bomb should explode
On that little school in Kensal Rise
At the end of Harvist Road

PRIVILEGE OF GENDER

When we look back through the ages
And history turns its pages
The balance of the gender is all wrong
With women never free
Of domesticity
And it was ever thus in days long gone

Women couldn't choose it
Those born with skill would lose it
Suppressed by all their duties as a wife
History on balance
Shows the wasting of their talents
As they coped with the unfairness of their life

Did Anne Hathaway manoeuvre
Poor Will to push the Hoover
As Shakespeare sat to write a famous play
And when he wrote a sonnet
Were bees buzzing in his bonnet
That he hadn't time to ink his quill today

Would da Vinci's brain start rusting
If he stopped to do the dusting
Stop inventing and attend to household chores
Should he de-frost the freezer
And not paint the Mona Lisa
And lose her enigmatic smile to gender laws

The Moulin Rouge gyrated
As Lautrec sat and painted
And watched the *femme de France* dance the can-can
But it wouldn't be the same
And the split of sex to blame
If Toulouse had been a woman – not a man

Great men stood complacent
While their womenfolk adjacent
Pandered to their every wish and whim
Would the Sistine Chapel glow
If Michelangelo
Had to paint the house and leave the cherubim

The female role on earth
Was to marry and give birth
The needs of all the children filled her heart
While men would paint and plaster
Play the 'Great I Am' and master
She didn't have the time for works of art

Now I've got to stop composing
The garden needs a hosing
There isn't time to ponder or to play
I must pause in my creating
There's a pile of washing waiting
And poetry must wait another day

RACE

James Cleveland (Jesse) Owens
12.9.13 – 31.3.80

There's egg on your face Mr Hitler
With your ideology
Highlighting a pure Aryan race
And German supremacy

Nineteen-thirty-six Olympic Games
Held that summer in Berlin
Didn't quite go as you planned
When a black man dared to win

Lined up with white contestants
Was a man of Negro birth
Soon to upset your grand design
He was the fastest guy on earth

Nicknamed 'The Buckeye Bullet'
This Afro-American
Won the long jump and the hurdles
And every race he ran

Born in Alabama
The grandson of a slave
Aged seven he picked cotton
And with his brothers played

And so Mein Fuhrer Adolph
When history is told
Despite your manic ravings
Jesse Owens won four Gold

RETURN TO SENDER

I used to like my postman
A happy little chap
With his pile of cheery letters
And his jaunty postman's cap

I'd watch him coming up the road
In his bright red anorak
Weighed down with post and parcels
In a rucksack on his back

But now my post is changing
It's unsolicited you see
Why are these depressing letters
Addressed to the likes of me

The first one that I open
From a charity 'that cares'
Is offering me a stair-lift
To help me up the stairs

A scooter for mobility
Well, I guess that wouldn't hurt
If they'd throw in a tartan blanket
To cover up my mini-skirt

There's 'easy access' to the shower
And I know that this sounds daft
They want to send a blooming hoist
To lift me out the bath

Each week I'm urged to write my will
And I'm told that in conjunction
I should appoint 'Power of Attorney'
For when my brain-cells cease to function

And today I've had this letter
Some unknown solicitor man
Offering burial or cremation
And a tax-free funeral plan

I'll send an answer to this dimwit
Say – When I give up the fight
I'll climb the highest mountain
Then combust and self-ignite

Can't stop to open any more
I'm on a ten-mile hike
After that I'll do three circuits
Round the lakeside on my bike

Then I'm going dancing
So why can't they offer me
A pair of red stilettos
With a high-life guarantee

Or how about a new bikini
Caribbean waters I will swim
And I'd like a letter telling me
Of a great big lottery win

I'm trekking China's Great Wall
I'll cruise the Amazon and back
And all your rotten letters
Will lay unopened on the mat

But I'll keep my sense of humour
And laugh – I guess it's funny
I'll refuse to leave this mortal coil
'Til I've spent all my money

Although this poem's jokey
And written in a huff
I don't want unasked for rubbish
And all this ageist stuff

And so my dearest postman
To old age I'll not surrender
And you can take these letters back
All marked 'Return to Sender'

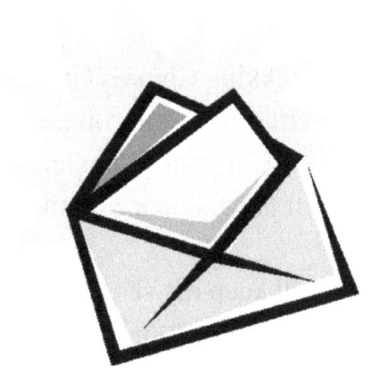

RITA AND TREVOR
August – Lloret de Mar

(Apologies to the English Language and to the Spanish!)

It's nice to come somewhere foreign
Costa Brava to Lloret de Mar
We've got a full week on a complex
And don't have to walk far for the bar

We've got a good deal – all inclusive
We don't have to cook or self-cater
And for our stay – the foods free all day
And we have our own Spanish waiter

What's this 'ere meat that we're eating
Is it right that in Spain they eat horse
Oi Pedro, I'll have pie and mash, mate
Mushy peas and a squirt of brown sauce

What's all this green stuff they've give us
Bring me black pudding and fries
And fish that is shaped into fingers
Not complete on a plate with its eyes

I don't fancy yer yella paella
It's full of octopussies and squid
What I want is a Lidl's pot noddle
Nip out and get two for a quid

Now I've lost the string on me tea-bag
It's as weak as the pee of a gnat
Oi Pedro, I'll have eggs and sausage
And make sure I get chips with that

Reet fancies a fizzy blue cocktail
Oi Pedro, por favor, can you 'ear
And fetch us a pack of pork scratchings
They'll go down a treat with me beer

They don't have real proper food here
The tapas and oil make me sick
It's all fresh figs and black olives
No treacle pudding or good spotted dick

We've had a whole week all inclusive
Here scorching in Lloret de Mar
I've worn me best cap with the peak at the back
And propped up the swimming pool bar

We've bingo and prize karaoke
And Reet's turn created a storm
She's gone and won us a package
Next year here in Spain's Benidorm

But we'd be better off down in Bognor
At that nice B & B – *Inglenook*
There's nothing wrong with the Spanish
They just haven't learned how to cook

Luv Rita and Trev

RITA AND TREVOR
July – Benidorm

(More apologies to the English Language and to the Spanish!)

I've won us this package vacation
Benidorm, karaoke's top prize
In Lloret de Mar – I sang like a star
My 'Delia' brought tears to their eyes

I've leopard print leggings from Primark
On the Costa we're spending two weeks
Trev can wear his gold chain – engraved with his name
I've had me hair done with pink streaks

He can wear his new T-shirt with slogans
His shorts with his sandals and socks
And with his fake tan – he'll be medallion man
And I'll wear me crimplene frocks

I've me bri-nylon blouse that is see-through
And me under-wired bra that is black
And, Trev, it won't hurt – if you take off your shirt
And show off the tattoos on your back

I've trousers in lime polyester
(They're elastic to hold in me fat)
With me teeth-whitened smile – they'll see I've got style
In me best Blackpool 'Kiss Me Quick' hat

It says here we must dress up for dinner
Real swanky, these posh hotel do's
Trev's got a string vest – to cover his chest
And I've got me green platform shoes

We'll drink sangria from flash glasses
I'll have a sparkler in mine
Oi Pedro, let's see ya – bring us more tequila
And a jug of that cheap Spanish wine

With me own plastic bed by the pool side
The chlorine fumes filling me head
Factor fifty sun-cream – a 'Hello' magazine
See me cellulite turn blotchy red

We tried all that flamenco dancing
'Til Trev, he could stand it no longer
And so to be fair – and let down their hair
He led them all off in a Conga

There's nothing much wrong with the Spanish
Me and Trevor could learn them some tricks
The dark senoritas – with flashing eyes greet us
But they ain't got the style of us Brits

Luv Rita and Trev

RITA AND TREVOR
September – France

(Even more apologies to the English language and to the French!)

Now that we're world travellers
(Well, twice we've been to Spain)
It's not all it's cracked up to be
So we won't go there again

Where shall we go on holiday
It's time we must decide
A B&B in Ilfracombe
Or that boarding house in Ryde

Trev switched off the telly
(He was watching sport on Sky)
How about we go to France
We could drive – no need to fly

There's a motorway to take us
Right down south to St. Tropez
We'll be heading for the sunshine
On the Autoroute Soleil

So I packed us some sandwiches
And a Thermos flask of tea
We crossed the English Channel
And stocked up on duty-free

We stopped at a French Café
On a nice 'Aire de Repos'
Trev looked at the menu
Said – I don't want none of those

I'll eat French fries and croissants
What's this – God only knows
I don't want frogs' legs in garlic
And they can keep their escargots

And when we left still starving
Trev gave us a nasty fright
He forgot that in this foreign place
They drive the wrong way on the right

The gendarme waved his gun about
Wrote a fine out on the spot
He took two hundred euros
Every single cent we'd got

Then we re-joined the motorway
But before a mile or two
I said – Trev can you stop the car
I'm bursting for the loo

I went into this centre
The smell led me to the door
But to my shocked amazement
Found a hole there in the floor

I found the place to put me feet
And balanced with precision
But with no free hand to hold me nose
Knew I'd made the wrong decision

I tried to pull me trousers down
And thought with some relief
That it was blooming lucky
I hadn't tights on underneath

I clutched me clothes around me knees
To keep them out the bowl
And tried to think of England
But me foot slipped down the hole

Fixed in a crouched position
Head held high and bottom low
But at this awkward angle
Me water-works won't flow

With me body all contorted
Bringing tears before me eyes
To keep a squatting balance
Ain't half painful on the thighs

Knickers bunched around me kneecaps
With a whoosh and in a rush
Water swirled around me ankles
From the automatic flush

I staggered to the car park
Said – Trev, these French are mental
He said – Reet, just dry your feet
It's because they're continental

Then I saw his face was smirking
I said – Don't you Rita me
I'll not go through this performance
Every time I want a wee

I said, Trev, I've got me standards
I'll not go there again
'Til the French have proper toilets
With bowls of porcelain

And so we did a U-turn
To the channel – crossed back over
I don't want to stay in St. Tropez
I'll spend two weeks in Dover

Luv Rita and Trev

SCOOTER-HOOTER JAILBIRDS

Sometimes I get angry
That there are those in jail
Better treated than the pensioners
Who are old and sick and frail

O.A.P's should come out fighting
The revolution's just begun
We can get ourselves arrested
If we block up the M1

So all of us with scooters
Join the rally and let's drive
Spread out across the motor-way
And 'scoot' up the M5

Over 60's Clubs from Basingstoke
Let loose and fancy free
Will head the scooter cavalcade
To block-up the M3

On the M4 from Wales to London
We will cause a mighty row
If we can block the motorway
From Maidenhead to Slough

Just think of all the chaos
If a scheme we can contrive
To isolate the capital
By circling the M25

Millions on mobility-scooters
Stretched across the motorways
Will bring the country to a stand-still
We can keep it up for days

With speeds of just eight miles an hour
Blasting with our scooter-hooters
As we re-charge at the 'Services'
And frustrate all the commuters

We can block-up the hard-shoulder
So no police cars would get through
At each junction we can organise
A mobile 'Portaloo'

And when motorists get angry
We'll ignore their mad tirades
Those with selective hearing
Will switch off their hearing-aids

We can paralyse the system
Gridlock the country far and wide
Rampaging pensioners on scooters
Abreast the motorways we'll ride

When the police come to arrest us
And charge us for our sins
We'll opt to go to prison
Where a better life begins

A prison doctor there on call
No more lengthy G.P. waits
No more gas and 'lecky' bills
Once we're inside those prison gates

We'll all demand our human rights
Peruse the menu – what to eat?
Nothing past its sell-by-date
Fresh fish and veg and meat

Three course meals served daily
And turkey Christmas Day
We'll all be laughing up our sleeves
As the poor tax-payers pay

Hot water, warmth and duvets
No more decisions – 'heat or eat'
And we can join the prison gym
To keep us fit and on our feet

A flat-screen telly in our cell
And all our washing done
We can have computer lessons
Play bingo and have fun

So now I've solved the problem
No expensive nursing home
We'll have prison staff to care for us
And an in-cell telephone

A guard to tuck us up in bed
And jailhouse rules explicit
They must bring hot water bottles
When our joints become arthritic

We'll use our time quite wisely
Have other prisoners to thank
Because the Hatton Garden mob
Will teach us how to rob a bank

Although this poem's fanciful
The picture it creates
Of scooter-hooter jailbirds
Rubbing shoulders with cell-mates

Many a true word said in jest
But wrong it must surely be
When thugs get treated better
Than the average O.A.P.

SEX IN H.D.

To the T.V. in the corner
I've made my feelings plain
With righteous indignation
I have switched it off again

There's same sex fornication
With sexy images obscene
And the writhing of mixed gender
On the television screen

With bumps and grunts and twanging
Of the bedsprings in H.D.
Bare bottoms bouncing up and down
Is all too much for me

You might think me old-fashioned
But with my last embarrassed cough
Just stop the world from spinning round
And Dear God let me get off

SHADOW

His silent presence won't release me
Elusive as the dawning mist
Chained to his censure I'm not free
My every movement he'll foresee
To haunt my footsteps he'll persist

His outline shimmers in the sunlit stream
On sandy beach and dusty street
On star-filled nights, in moonlight's beam
Furtive as the darkest dream
Silent as his image meets my feet

He waits for me 'neath the dull street light
'Though fast I run and fear I show
This cold grey man who fuels my flight
He abandons me on the blackest night
My conscience and my shadow

This type of five line poem is called a Cinquain
and dates back to medieval French poetry
(Also called Quintain)
Lines 1, 3 & 4 rhyme, as do lines 2 & 5

SNOW-LIGHT

Iridescent shimmer of elusive light
Mystical beams on snow-covered ground
From a pain-tangled tunnel, dark as night
To crystal filled radiance, star-spangled bright
And the song of angels all around

Those passed before me in ethereal state
Happy laughter in soft sparkling snow
With welcoming arms, for me they wait
And all my earthly fears abate
In the countenance of angels' glow

Nurses bustle, but they do not see
Curtains swish and bed-pans clang
But cold, untouched, my morning tea
In peace I rest, but my spirit's free
Last night I played snow-balls … and angels sang

SPRING FORWARD

Spring forward into happiness
Make time to have some fun
Spring forward into laughter
And when that's gone and done

Old age will never blight you
You'll re-live memories of the past
Fall back on years of yesterday
'Til the clock has ticked its last

Spring forward into Summer-time
To Greenwich Mean plus one
The sunny days stretch far ahead
As we embrace the warming sun

But come the end of Autumn
When cold winds chill the air
Jack Frost paints our windows
And of leaves the trees are bare

Then fall back into Winter days
Warm fires and mistletoe
The earth becomes a wonderland
Diamonds sparkle in the snow

Live life like the seasons
In tune with nature's charm
Blossom in the morning sun
And rest with night-time's calm

The clock hands keep on ticking
With nature's seasonal rhyme
Spring forward into Summer
And fall back at Winter time

THE AGE OF LONELINESS

Each night as I lay in my bed
And quietly shed a tear
There's an empty space beside me
No-one to love and to hold dear

Too frail now to venture
Outside to join the throng
In a neglected generation
And a society gone wrong

Although my body's weakening
My mind is clear and sharp
But logging on the internet
Won't gladden my sad heart

I switch on my computer
Find junk mails by the score
As the postman pushes circulars
About pizzas through my door

I'm on Facebook and on Twitter
I've a WhatsApp on my 'phone
But I need someone to speak to
As I live each day alone

From the store where 'Every Little Helps'
I buy groceries on line
My weekly shop the driver drops
But he's too rushed to pass the time

The 'phone pierces my silence
And a 'scammers' voice I hear
He speaks with foreign accent
And I hold my breath in fear

Head blurred with words unspoken
No-one will ever hear
No smile to fill the endless day
No laughter to bring cheer

A garden overgrown with weeds
Beyond my tender care
No more happy sunlit days
And glass of wine to share

No neighbours there with friendly face
Each home has working wives
As husbands sweat and children fret
Immersed in busy lives

I'm old, alone, invisible
Not worth the time of day
With the harshness of reality
I'm a burden – in the way

No-one has time to bother
But is that an excuse
To treat the older generation
As if they're of little use

And so I'll moulder sadly
Unheard, ignored, unseen
Amidst a life that shuns the old
And dream a lonely dream

The scourge of modern living
Is the loneliness of age
As I wait in God's Waiting Room
To turn the final page

TREE OF KNOWLEDGE

Learning is a beautiful thing
No-one can take away
As through life we gather knowledge
Hour by hour and day by day
From the time of struggle at our birth
Little fingers learn to grasp
To appreciate security
In our mother's warming clasp

We find our voice with first a cry
And then we learn to talk
From gently guided footsteps
On life's journey start to walk
Sheltered years when we beguile
With innocence and winning smile
In each and every one of us
An individual style

And then the break with mother
When we learn that school days bring
Independence and a structure
And a thing called discipline
And if we learn the latter
And do as our teachers tell
From the fountain of their knowledge
We can fill the deepest well

We go to university
And examination passes show
The subjects we have studied
Lead to where we want to go
We forge the ties of friendship
And with interwoven schemes
Sow the seeds of our ambition
On the horizon of our dreams

Then hurled into the working world
Competitive and hard
A small fish in a big pond
Or in a pack we're just a card
And still we go on learning
A career to forge ahead
Life's challenging diversity
Down pathways we are led

Some may reach the pinnacle
Others be a vital cog
But shun the discipline of learning
And we'll just be the underdog
We earn our keep for forty years
Work too should be enjoyed
Each day to thank our lucky stars
We're healthy and employed

And when we reach retirement
And life once again becomes our own
Rejoice in acquired knowledge
Our ageing brain-cells to re-hone
We've seen our children prosper
Nurtured with our loving care
And passed on to them the wisdom
That just the old can share

If we've lived our lives with open minds
Receptive, wise and strong
Grasped at opportunity
Made mistakes both right and wrong
The discipline of learning
If in this we all believe
Embrace the tree of knowledge
And life's rewards achieve

TUNE ON A TAMBOURINE

It's now a distant memory
But I recall the scene
Of all the little children
Dancing on the village green
Of maypole ribbons twirling
And voices sweet in sound
The gaily painted horses
Of the old merry-go-round

The farmers winning rosettes
For their livestock proudly shown
The competition for the best and
Biggest vegetables they'd grown
A time of simple pleasures
A day old folk sit and dream
And the gypsy played a merry tune
On a well-worn tambourine

No-one saw the sky was darkening
No-one heard the fateful drone
As an aircraft called a Messerschmitt
Made its lonely way back home
With machine guns spitting venom
Bombs unleashed from its hold
The killing of the children
The burning horror to unfold

In deathly aftermath, the agony
The wailing out of grief
The crater where the maypole stood
Now viewed with disbelief
The time was nineteen-forty-two
And I still hear each scream
And the echo of the gypsy's tune
On a silent tambourine

WHAT'S IN A NAME

Walking, working and What's 'is Name
The majors in my life
The first two bring me pleasure
The third one causes strife

Walking brings serenity
Emerald fields, the river's flow
And working pays the money
To make my nest egg grow

But What's 'is Name brings meaning
Love and laughter to my life
And I'll treasure that for ever
As Mrs What's 'is Name, his wife

Why do I call him What's 'is Name?
Pause a moment to reflect
It's our nearest and our dearest
We're most likely to neglect

With all our friends and colleagues
We're patient and polite
It's to those who are the closest
That we snap and snarl and fight

So let's redress the balance
No more voices raised in blame
I'll suffer on in silence
With my Mr What's 'is Name

WILDEBEEST FEAST

Leo went shopping in Asda
In Tesco's and Sainsbury's too
He needed a rare cut of zebra
Or meat to make antelope stew

He wanted to cook a nice dinner
For his wife – the queen of the pride
With ingredient list at the ready
Nothing too good for his bride

The buffalo section was empty
Of elephant shops were bereft
No kangaroo – he searched the shop through
And of crocodile nothing was left

He thought of a nice hippo hot-pot
Or leg of giraffe he could braise
He wanted to cook his wife's dinner
To win back her favour and praise

His mate had never been happy
Urban jungles did not suit Louise
She yearned for the African sunshine
And monkeys that swing through the trees

So Leo and Lou headed homeward
Where lions prey on wild wildebeest
And back with the pride in the jungle
Celebrate with a wildebeest feast

<u>WRITE IT MY WAY</u>

To write like famous poets
In the style that they compose
Is a task that I've been given
But how to do it – goodness knows

I tried to copy Shakespeare
But each quiver of the quill
Soon had me catatonic
Acting like a sleeping pill

I tried to write like Wordsworth
As I'm fond of daffodils
But though I wandered as a cloud
I haven't got the skills

I thought a bit of Betjeman
And his desire to drop a bomb
Don't know why he picked on Slough
Or where that thought came from

I'll never be a Barrett-Browning
Writing *'How Do I Love Thee'*
Rudyard Kipling, Percy Shelley
Clever words that are not me

Even boxers get poetic
Like the heavy-weight Ali
When he was *'Floating Like a Butterfly*
And Stinging Like A Bee'

I could go back through the ages
Lord Tennyson or Blake
But to copy these great masters
Would be a big mistake

Philip Larkin, Dylan Thomas
Recorded for posterity
Chaucer, Keats or Roald Dhal
Names esteemed in history

But I'll never be a Poet Laureate
My name won't list among the great
But my funny little verses
I'll still happily create

I've always liked the Pam Ayres style
Her words make people laugh
So I'll write my rhyming drivel
Nothing clever – mostly daft

I've decided that I'll write like me
With just a dash of Pam
And I'll compose my poetry
My style – the way I am